D1559111

THE
TRACK & FIELD
PSYCHOLOGY
WORKBOOK

"From Average to Primetime"

Attain the Mental Edge

DEDICATION

This Workbook is specially dedicated to all the young Track and Field Stars of the world. With relentless pursuit, undying passion, and laser focus even your wildest dreams can become a reality.

PREFACE

In todays' track and field world there are (overall) 4 types of athletes. Here's what those are:

1. *Talented Athletes* who are *Ambitious* to Learn how to Improve
2. *Non-Talented Athletes* who are *Ambitious* to Learn how to Improve
3. *Talented Athletes* who have *No Ambition* to Learn how to Improve
4. *Non-Talented Athletes* who have *No Ambition* to Learn how to Improve

Being born with Talent or Not is something that is really out of the Athlete's control... but having the Ambition to Learn and Improve is completely something that we have the power to influence. Why do I make this a point? Because many of the track and field athletes now and days get caught up in the idea that Talent automatically equals success during competition. That Talent is the answer to all problems. That Talent makes it "Easy." That Talent nearly guarantees the college scholarship everyone is after...And this couldn't be further from the truth. Although Talent does predispose some athletes to be more skilled and enables them to learn a lot faster than others....the truth is that the real reason athletes become successful is because they possess the ambition to learn and improve and actually go out and put in the work! It is 1000% possible for an athlete to have zero track and field talent but work their tail off to achieve massive success.

However, with that being said let's get something straight right off the bat. If you're picking up this workbook with the expectation of finding some sort of short-cut...some sort of secret formula...some sort of magic potion you can use that will allow you to bypass all the hard work and effort that's required to become successful, you're simply Wasting Your Time! You won't find it here and you won't find it anywhere else, because it just doesn't exist.

The fact is that without the Ambition to Learn and Improve and the Desire to put in the work your results will continue to be mediocre. And our aim isn't for you to be a mediocre athlete. In fact, this Workbook is geared specifically to those of you in the 1st and 2nd quadrants only, meaning whether you are naturally talented or not you're without question eager to work hard and eager to learn how you can get better in any way, shape, or form.

Now, for purposes of clarity this workbook has one goal, and only one goal in mind: TO IMPROVE YOUR TRACK AND FIELD PERFORMANCE. How will we accomplish this? Well, we will do this by showing you how your thoughts and mindset have a direct impact on how well you perform on the track or field. We will give you deep insight as to how your inner emotions and thoughts can leave you vulnerable to consistently under-performing which in turn can lead to anger, frustration, and disappointment. Along the way, you will learn the mental skills that many of today's great athletes use to propel themselves ahead of their competition. You will learn what it takes to perform your best under intense pressure, you will learn how to overcome crippling adversity, you will learn how to cope with pre-match nerves and anxiety, you will build mental toughness, and you will learn to develop supreme confidence in your abilities. As the rest of the world is just now realizing "Physical Skills are important, but Mental Skills are what separates Champions from the Rest of the Pack."

TABLE OF CONTENTS

- How will Mental Imagery Influence my Athletic Performance?

4. **Thought Suppression**: "The Truth of the Matter is that Thought Suppression is a Lot Like Not Studying Before a Big Test, You're Simply Setting Yourself Up for Failure"

   - What is Thought Suppression?
   - How does Thought Suppression impact my track and field performances?
   - What are some strategies to avoid Suppressing my Thoughts?

5. **Competitive Anxiety**: "You Never Reach your Full Potential because you Let Fear Control your Thoughts, and those Fearful Thoughts Create Fearful Emotions, and those Fearful Emotions Lead to Fearful Actions"

   - What is Competitive Anxiety?
   - How does Competitive Anxiety affect athletes differently?
   - How can I learn to control my Anxiety to perform better?

6. **Self-Talk**: "Self-Talk has been Shown to be an Incredibly Powerful Psychological Skill that is Used by Some of the Most Successful Track and Field Athletes"

   - What is Self-Talk?
   - How can Self-Talk help me perform better on the track or field?

- What are the different types of Self-Talk?

7. **Zones of Optimal Performance**: "Reaching a Mental Zone is Difficult, but When Accomplished Many Athletes Describe the Ease of Winning Competitions, Defeating Opponents Feels Like Taking Candy from a Baby, and Every Move Becomes Buttery Smooth"

   - What is a Zone of Optimal Performance?
   - Where is my level of Optimal Performance?
   - What skills can I utilize to reach my Zone of Optimal Performance?

8. **Attention**: "With so Many Factors Fighting for Your Attention You Become Like a Sniper in the Middle of a Warzone, You Need to be Able to Focus All of Your Attentive Energy on the Things that Matter Most at that Very Moment"

   - What are the different forms of Attention?
   - Why do I have Mental lapses and Attentive break downs?
   - What can I do to have laser like focus?

9. **Self-Confidence**: "You are the Architect, you can Build Yourself Up High Like a SkyScraper or you can set a Flimsy Foundation that can Collapse at any Moment."

   - How can I Build up my Self-Confidence?
   - What are the different factors that can influence my Self-Confidence?

- How can I sustain high levels of Confidence throughout the course of my track and field career?

10. **Coming Back From Injury**: "What Most Athletes Fail to Realize is that the Physical Pain is Intense, but Tolerable, it's the Psychological Pain that Becomes Almost Unbearable to Deal With"

- What are the Psychological factors involved in Injury Recovery?
- How can I return from an Injury faster and stronger than before?
- What are the Physical and Psychological connections when an Injury occurs?

Motivation

> *"A TRACK & FIELD ATHLETE WITHOUT MOTIVATION IS LIKE A CAR WITHOUT GAS, NEITHER WILL GET VERY FAR."*

Mental Meltdown

You're waking up out of bed, 7:00am sharp on a cold December morning. The entire week you've been motivated about becoming a better sprinter and leading up to today you've made the conscious decision to wake up early, put your running shoes on, grab your bag, and head straight down to the track to work on your sprinting technique. But now that the day has finally arrived... you realize that it's Saturday, it's cold, your body is sore from yesterday's practice, and you're just way too warm and comfortable in your bed at the moment to get up and start your workouts. You hit snooze on the alarm and go back to sleep.

What happen to the overflowing amounts of Motivation you had?

Now let's not get carried away, athletes go through these situations all the time and under certain circumstances it's perfectly okay to get some extra rest. After all the grind of a competitive season brings along a lot of stress on the body that requires some recovery and recuperation time. It only becomes a problem when skipping workouts and not following through with your commitments becomes a habit. And unfortunately this is very, and I mean very, common. Just take a listen to some of the promises your friends and peers make when summer time comes around... "I'm going to lose 20 pounds and get my body summer ready... I'm going to diet and eat nothing but fruits and vegetables for the next two weeks... I'm going to wake up early every day and go to the gym."

Fast forward to a few months later and guess what? Absolutely nothing has changed! No diet, no weight loss, and of course no early morning gym sessions. To get to the point, without a true sense of motivation it becomes extremely difficult to get things done. And when you're an aspiring athlete this makes all the difference. To become successful on the track or field it's crucial that you identify what your underlying motivation is so that you can feed off of it and use it to fuel your efforts.

 ## Definition & Examples

Motivation: your "reason", your "why" of what you practice for and what you work hard for.

Example

1. "I'm staying late after practice today to work on my sprinting technique." Why am I staying late? Because I want to be a better sprinter than my older brother. So my motivation is beating and performing better than my older brother.

   Little Known Fact: Motivation as a whole goes a whole lot deeper, and here's a quick breakdown. There are actually two different types of motivation... Intrinsic Motivation and Extrinsic Motivation.

Intrinsic Motivation: motivation that comes from within you or from inside of you.

Example

1. "I have a passion and a love for sprinting. I don't need any extra attention from people or any special prizes to keep competing, I simply enjoy being part of the sport."

Extrinsic Motivation: motivation that comes from something outside of you.

1. "I like to sprint because it makes my dad really happy. Also, for every competition that I win I get a crisp $20 bill, this keeps me driven to perform my best.

Intrinsic　　Vs　　Extrinsic

The Game Plan

Simple distinction right? If you didn't understand the difference between the two types please take a moment and re-read both definitions and examples again. Now, you might be wondering which type of motivation is best for maximizing your talents and efforts? And if you guessed Intrinsic Motivation, you are Correct. Here's why.

When your motivation comes from within you, you don't need some external reward or some type of trophy to work hard and give it your all. It's just something that comes natural to you, and you feel a burning desire inside of you to continue to push yourself. You have a passion and a love for track and field, and if you receive anything along the way it's nice to get the recognition but it's not necessary for you to continue to be driven. And the truth is that this is the way most really successful track and field athletes maintain high levels of performance. When you're watching your favorite competitors on TV this is difficult to notice because of course they are under the spot light and have all the attention from fans, but what you don't see is the thousands and thousands of hours of practice that go on behind the scenes. And it's no surprise that the best athletes are the same ones who are last to leave the gym and practice fields, despite them already knowing they are better than everyone else.

Now on the other hand, when an athlete is Extrinsically Motivated, they may find success in the beginning… but what eventually ends up happening is their motivation starts to slowly fade away which only leads to the athlete "burning out." If you're not familiar with the term Burn Out, it's simply a term used to describe the physical and mental exhaustion of an athlete. Why does this happen? Well, this type of athlete works hard also, but only works hard for the reward, works hard for the trophy, works hard for the scholarship, works hard for the money. Once the athlete acquires these external objects that he/she is motivated in attaining, what's next? What comes after that? What becomes their reason for continued hard work and effort? NOTHING! There aren't any other reasons or desires to want to continue to improve and get better. Since this athlete's sole motivation was to possess that external reward, once it's in their hands they become complacent, comfortable, and un-driven. With that being said, there's no problem with getting recognition for athletic achievement…it's actually something to be extremely proud of and something that should be celebrated. The issue only becomes apparent if you're true underlying goal is to become the BEST.

If I don't win 1st Place this season I won't compete anymore

Whether I win or lose, I will continue to compete because I love the sport

So what's the take away? In order to be successful in track and field you need to find your true Intrinsic Motivation. Find your Why. Find your reason. And make sure it's something that makes YOU happy, NOT someone else. Keep that fire inside of you burning for as long as possible, because once it's gone it's very hard to get it lit again.

Mental Workout

1. Write down all the reasons why you compete in track & field. What's your motivation for competing? Is it Intrinsic or Extrinsic?

_____

_____

_____

_____

_____

_____

2. Write down all the reasons why you think you feel motivated one day, and unmotivated the next day. What types of distractions do you have around you? How can you avoid these distractions from getting in the way of your success?

_____

_____

_____

_____

_____

_____

_____

3. Talk to your friends and teammates and see if you can find what drives their motivation. Can you tell who is Extrinsically Motivated and who is Intrinsically Motivated?

_____

_____

_____

_____

_____

_____

_____

_____

Goal-Setting

"NOT SETTING GOALS IS LIKE PLAYING A GAME WITHOUT KEEPING SCORE, YOU CAN'T REALLY TELL WHETHER YOU'RE WINNING OR LOSING."

Mental Meltdown

Imagine this… You wake up from a long nap and find yourself alone in a car with no phone or any type of technology in sight. You're headed on a long road trip to a small town that you know is somewhere to the North of you but you have no directions as to how to get there. You really have no idea how far this place is or how long it should take you to get there.

What are you to do?

This example is a little far-fetched (as you will probably never be put in this position), but it makes the perfect point: YOU CAN'T REALLY KNOW WHERE YOU'RE GOING WITHOUT A CLEAR ROADMAP! And a goal is exactly that, a roadmap to reach your desired level of success. For some odd reason however, many of today's youth athletes really have no desire to create clear and concise goals. Which leads to the questions… Where are you going? How will you get there? When will you get there? What do you need in order to arrive on time?

The Best Athletes know what they want, they understand exactly what it will take to get there, and they know how long it will take them to get there. It's not a very complicated process to understand, but there are some key factors you need to be aware of in terms of learning proper goal setting techniques. Once you get these strategies down, you'll be light years ahead of your peers and will drastically improve your chances of success!

Definition & Examples

Goal- the end result of something you are targeting or trying to accomplish.

Example

1. "My goal is to be the best high jumper I can be."

Most of the goals you set for yourself are very likely similar to the example given above. Really simple, really generic, and straight to the point. But there's a huge problem with setting goals this way. What's the problem? These types of goals never get accomplished! They never get accomplished because there's no way of measuring any type of progress. Setting a very vague goal doesn't give you the ability to track whether or not you're taking steps forward, taking steps backwards, or staying in the exact same place. The simple solution to this requires the athlete to become more specific, which leads us to our next point...there are two categories when it comes to goal setting: short term goals and long term goals.

Long Term Goal- your main objective/target. (big picture)

Short Term Goal- checkpoints that need to be reached in order to accomplish your long term goal. (small scope)

Example

1. "Two months from now I want to increase the amount of weight I can squat at my max by 40 pounds, that's my long-term goal. In order to do that I need to increase the amount of weight I can squat at my max by 20 pounds every month, which breaks down into an increase of about 5 pounds per week, those are my short-term goals. In order to increase the amount of weight I can squat at my max by 5 pounds every week I'm going to do squats every other day after practice and I'm going to keep track of how many sets I do as well as how much weight I can add to the bar (even more precise short term goals)." The more precise you get, the better.

Week 1

Monday	Tuesday	Wednesday	Thursday	Friday
3 sets of 4 reps at 140lbs		3 sets of 4 reps at 140lbs		2 sets of 3 reps at 145lbs

Overall= increase of 5lbs

Week 2

Monday	Tuesday	Wednesday	Thursday	Friday
2 sets of 3 reps at 145lbs		2 sets of 4 reps at 145lbs		3 sets of 2 reps at 150lbs

Overall= increase of 5lbs

Week 3

Monday	Tuesday	Wednesday	Thursday	Friday
2 sets of 3 reps at 150lbs		3 sets of 2 reps at 150lbs		1 set of 2 reps at 155lbs

Overall= increase of 5lbs

Week 4

Monday	Tuesday	Wednesday	Thursday	Friday
1 set of 2 reps at 150lbs		2 sets of 2 reps at 150lbs		1 set of 1 rep at 160lbs

Overall= increase of 5lbs

The Game Plan

Okay let's quickly recap. You need to set a long term goal (destination) along with short term goals (specific directions) to help you reach your target level of success. Simple. now let's take it one step further. Whenever you set a long term or short term goal you need to make sure that it's not Too Easy, but not Impossibly Difficult. The level of difficulty that every goal should fall between is right around the moderately difficult category. Take a look at the spectrum that follows.

Goal Setting Level of Difficulties

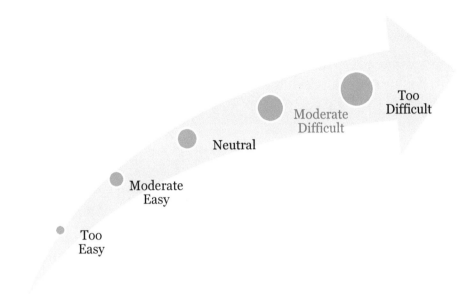

Too Easy- Not at all challenging for you

Moderately Easy- Only a little challenging for you

Neutral- An even balance between easy and challenging for you

Moderately Difficult- Challenging and pushes your Limits

Too Difficult- Overly challenging and difficult to notice any real progress

The magic formula lands in the moderately difficult category for the simple reason that these types of goals challenge you and test your limits but also give you a certain sense of belief that you can accomplish what you've set out to accomplish. Let's consider the other side of the coin. When a goal is too easy it doesn't challenge or motivate you which leads to boredom, and when a goal is extremely difficult it's really hard for you to see any results or progress. Without seeing any results or progress your confidence is shot down to the ground, and will eventually lead to you quitting or giving up. That's the last thing we want.

Finally, something that you absolutely must remember from now on every time you set a goal should incorporate the following characteristics. The acronym is SMART. Here's what it stands for:

Specific: every goal you set must be very specific, clear, and concise.

Measurable: every goal you set must have some measurable aspect to it. If you're looking to become faster you can time yourself, if you want to get stronger you can keep track of how much weight you're lifting.

Action-oriented: every goal should require you to take action whether physically or mentally.

Realistic- as we mentioned before your goals need to be realistic (in the moderately difficult category, not impossibly difficult or incredibly easy).

Timely- all goals need to have a deadline, some sort of time frame to ensure you're doing everything you can to reach your target.

And there you have it, the Proper Goal Setting Techniques. By incorporating all facets: Long Term Goals, Short Term Goals, The Goal Setting Difficulty Spectrum, and SMART...you are equipped to improve your performance to a very high level at a very quick pace. And remember, as you begin to accomplish the goals you've set things will become easier and easier for you, allowing you to modify your goals as you go which will only make you that much better as an athlete.

 ental Workouts

1. Begin now, write down 3 long term goals you want to accomplish.

_____

_____

_____

_____

_____

_____

_____

_____

_____

_____

_____

2. Develop a plan and a series of short term goals of how you will accomplish those 3 long term goals. Remember to keep track, whether daily, weekly, or monthly.

_____

_____

_____

_____

_____

_____

_____

_____

_____

_____

_____

_____

Mental Imagery

"MENTAL IMAGERY IS A LITTLE LIKE HAVING A MOVIE IN YOUR HEAD, AND SIMPLY HITTING PLAY ON YOUR DVD PLAYER WHENEVER YOU'RE READY TO WATCH IT."

Mental Meltdown

There's nothing like watching one of those classic and exciting track and field movies. From Without Limits, to Saint Ralph, to Chariots of Fire, Unbroken, Running Brave, and list can go and on... There's just something special about watching a movie about the sport you love that motivates you to get back on the track or field and work your tail off! This may be in part due to the fact that so many of us consciously or unconsciously put ourselves in the role of the main characters in the movie. We take a ride on the emotional roll-a-coaster the film is portraying... we feel the pain, we feel the anguish, we feel the frustration, and at the end we feel the triumph and success when the movie characters pull it together and get the Win in the face of Adversity.

And in actuality, this exact process is a lot how Mental Imagery (also known as Visualization) works! Mental Imagery is like having a movie in your head, and simply hitting Play on the DVD player whenever you're ready to watch it.

Unlike the movies however, in real life things don't always end the way you'd want them to end. For example, after having a bad round or not performing up to your standards you may think back and begin to run all the costly mistakes you made during the course of the competition or across the entire season. You visualize yourself not being able to get over the hurdles, not exploding off the starting blocks, forgetting the game plan and strategy, getting frustrated, getting yelled at, being made fun of, and losing your place on the team despite all your hard work and effort. And in doing so you get yourself into a huge "funk" which is the exact opposite of what you wanted in the first place! In order to avoid this from happening, it's crucial you realize that the images you play in your head have an enormously powerful impact on your track and field performance. Learning the proper way to utilize Mental Imagery is vital, and it's important you use it as an advantage instead of as a pitfall so your ability can reap the positive benefits.

Definition & Example

Mental Imagery (Visualization)- using your thought processes and imagination to create very detailed images and pictures in your mind. These images can be of past experiences or future moments in the way you would like them to play out.

Example

1. I'm in the backyard practicing my shot put technique. I close my eyes and imagine placing the shot put on my neck. I get into my gliding position, the crowd is roaring, I can feel the pressure, but I'm confident. I explode off my backfoot, turn my body and pivot, gather momentum, and release the shot put with all my power and strength. The best throw of the day! The crowd goes wild, my teammates are jumping up and down with excitement, I can feel the adrenaline running through my veins, I won the match!

LIGHTS....CAMERA.... ACTION!!

The Game Plan

If you're aspiring to be a great track and field athlete at some point, then you've most definitely closed your eyes and dreamed about experiencing massive success on the competitive field... about leaving your opponents in the dust... about accomplishing incredible come from behind victories.... and gaining all the respect from your friends and peers. And it's perfectly normal, all great athletes do it regardless of the sport they participate in. What's important however is to realize that the way you process these mental images must be done in an effective and efficient manner. Believe it or not, there is a certain science to it. Here is a check list of components you need to use in order to apply Mental Imagery to your track and field career and maximize your potential.

Before working on your jump technique, before lifting weights, before competing in a tournament, anything that requires a specific skill set or process, take ten minutes and just visualize yourself being successful. Visualize yourself correctly executing every move, every movement, and every step. Imagine yourself flawlessly jumping over the high bar and setting a new personal record, being so fast that no one can run past you, being so strong that whatever weight you put on the bar seems light. You're just overflowing with confidence and can handle anything that comes your way. Along this process however, it's important that you be very, and I mean very detailed and specific on the pictures you're running through your mind. Like I mentioned earlier, it should be like playing a movie in your head.

You must use all your senses: touch, sight, smell, hear, taste. As you begin to learn how to incorporate all your senses, you will start to notice that you will progressively feel more and more as if you were presently in the moment you are imagining. And this is what we're aiming for. Because you're envisioning vivid and detailed mental pictures your brain begins to release the exact same chemicals and signals throughout your body as if you were actually in that moment. This will allow you to experience the same emotional responses and phenomenon's you would have as if it were happening in real time, thus allowing you to prepare in advance and give you the feeling as if "You've been there before" when that moment finally arrives.

Example:

Let's say that during last week's javelin throw competition you came in last place. You know you can perform much better, so before today's competition you take ten minutes and visualize yourself successfully executing your routine and throwing the javelin as far as you possibly can.... "I grab the javelin with a fork grip, I can feel the cold sweat drenched onto my jersey, I can hear the crowd chanting my name, I can smell and almost taste the popcorn coming from the snack bar, but my eyes are locked in on my target. I hold the javelin over my right shoulder...and I go through my usual routine...accelerate toward the throwing line, cross my right leg over, firmly plant my left, and pull the javelin back as far as I can. I throw the javelin with a nice high and tight release, and follow through completely ...the javelin smoothly glides through the air and falls at a distance surpassing my personal record." And repeat this same process again and again throw after throw...elevating your confidence each step of the way.

Learning how to become efficient in the use of mental imagery can be very challenging at times because it's not something that will give you immediate results. So it's important to remember that just like every other skill you've ever learned, you only get better with dedicated time and practice. When you were a baby and first started to learn how to walk it didn't just take you 1 day, it took you weeks, even months to learn how to execute every movement correctly. Don't get discouraged or frustrated in your beginning stages of mental imagery practice, even if you feel like it's not working. Keep practicing, keep getting better, and in time your performance will in fact positively benefit.

Mental Workout

1. Follow the steps given in the last few paragraphs. Take a skill you want to be better at, and before practicing or even during practice, envision yourself being successful. Picture yourself doing everything right. Remember to be very specific, think about all the steps, all the movements, and everything around you.

_____

_____

_____

_____

_____

_____

_____

_____

_____

_____

2. Once you start learning how mental imagery can work for you, start developing a routine. Maybe there's a quiet place that you can visit, a song you can play on your ipod, or a certain time of day when visualizing is more effective for you (in the morning when you wake up, or at night before you go to sleep). Repeat that routine as often as possible. Write your routine down.

_____

_____

_____

_____

_____

_____

_____

_____

_____

Thought Suppression

> *"THE TRUTH OF THE MATTER IS THAT THOUGHT SUPPRESSION IS A LOT LIKE NOT STUDYING BEFORE A BIG TEST, YOU'RE SIMPLY SETTING YOURSELF UP FOR FAILURE."*

Mental Meltdown

You're sprinting down the lane pole in hand quickly approaching the takeoff spot. You hit your top speed and begin to prepare to plant the pole into the box to engage in your jump. All you have to do is be consistent with your technique and you'll easily get up and over the crossbar, it's something you've done a million times in practice. However…as you gather your steps and take flight…your toe just slightly drags along the ground which affects your elevation and trajectory. Your concentration breaks for a split second but you try and compensate by arching your body earlier to help get you over the bar but it doesn't work…you simply couldn't get enough height on your jump and hit the crossbar squarely. Your team loses the competition and loses its playoff birth. On the bus ride home you can't help but have the same recurring thought run clear across your mind…

"I DON'T WANT TO THINK ABOUT IT ANYMORE!"

It happens to the best of us…all we want to do is bury that unforgiving memory into the deepest and darkest crevice of our mind and lock it away forever and ever…never to be seen again.

We want to get as far away as possible from those traumatizing and overwhelming feelings of despair, frustration, and disappointment.

This type of thought process is called Thought Suppression and it's exactly what many athletes engage in after a poor performance. But is Thought Suppression an effective strategy? Is Thought Suppression the best approach to overcoming a bad performance? What is the result of suppressing your thoughts? Well, in reality Thought Suppression is mentally one of the worst things you can possibly do when it comes to trying to elevate your athletic performance. It's really a lot like not studying before a big test, you're simply setting yourself up for failure.

Definition and Examples

Thought Suppression- attempting to stop thinking about a certain idea, or trying to stop certain thoughts from running through your mind.

Example

1. Let's further consider the same example given in the previous section. You were unable to get up and over the crossbar and are now on a very long bus ride home. You continue to have the same recurring thought "DON'T THINK ABOUT IT!!!"

The next day comes and you're still trying your best not to think about it. To aid the process, you try something a little different... every time those unwanted thoughts of the pole vaulting competition resurface into your consciousness, you attempt to replace those thoughts with other memories that are completely unrelated and unattached. You think about the amazing flavors of your favorite food...you think about your exciting upcoming family vacation...and you think about how nicely those new Jordan shoes fit you. (things that usually help you feel better)

And guess what??? This is where things get a little confusing, because what starts to happen is that now the unpleasant memory of the pole vaulting competition becomes linked to your pleasant memories of your favorite food, your family vacation, and your new Jordan shoes. Meaning that every time you think about these pleasant memories…your mind reverts back to not getting over the crossbar!

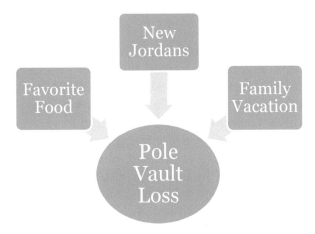

It's difficult to comprehend how this works in the beginning, but it's a very common phenomenon in psychology known as a Rebound Effect.

Thought Suppression Rebound Effect- as you attempt to suppress a thought (not think about it), you actually end up thinking about it even more. Your mind becomes occupied with thinking about the very thought you don't want to think about!

The Game Plan

Since it's a contradicting concept, let's explain in further detail. The way memory works in your mind is by forming links between associated objects or ideas. For example, when someone says the word "dog" what automatically pops into your head? You probably start to think about the words "paws, bark, bite, and fur." The stronger the links are between the associated objects or ideas, the higher likelihood you are to recall those particular memories. And since your mind doesn't distinguish between unwanted memories versus pleasant memories, when it comes to suppressing your thoughts and attempting to replace an unwanted memory with a pleasant memory you're actually associating and forming a bond/link between the two. And this is important to understand as a track and field athlete or an athlete in general because "DON'T THINK ABOUT IT" often leads to the exact opposite of what your desired goal is...which is to get over your poor performance or embarrassing moment. This begs the question.. if not thinking about it doesn't lead to your desired result, what can you do instead that'll help you overcome your mistake?

There are many possible solutions out there, but one stands out above all others....and it's called the *Mindfulness* approach. You might have heard of the term Mindfulness at some point in your early career or possibly even on Television, as professional athletes are slowly realizing its potential. Elva Dryer (two-time Olympian marathon runner representing the Unites States in 2000 and 2004) is a popular figure who used mindfulness techniques to improve her performance during competition. Entire books and numerous articles have been written about mindfulness and several studies have been conducted showing its positive effects which are being recognized by sports organizations all around the world. To get to the point however...Mindfulness is simply a word to describe a state of mind where you allow yourself to experience any and all thoughts you have and simply choose to view them in a non-judgmental manner. You're able to accept that thoughts are neither good or bad, but simply a natural process of human life. Mindfulness allows you to experience the moment in its entirety, and allows you to accept whatever has happened. Specifically in terms of track and field, you need to understand that there will be ups and downs and no athlete is an exception to this no matter how good they might be. Mistakes are going to happen and in no way should you allow them to haunt you as you try and move forward with your career. So in the event that you find yourself engaging in Thought Suppression, quickly become aware and implement more of a Mindfulness perspective into your thought process. Your experience as a track and field athlete will undoubtedly become much more enjoyable and much more successful.

 ental Workout

1.   Next time you compete, try to keep track of the thoughts that impact your performance negatively. Write some of these thoughts down below.

_____

_____

_____

_____

_____

_____

_____

_____

_____

_____

_____

_____

_____

2. Look at your list above. Are these thoughts a result of a negative experiences you've had in the past? Explain.

_____

_____

_____

_____

_____

_____

_____

_____

_____

_____

_____

_____

_____

_____

3. How will you use the Mindfulness approach immediately to
    keep you from suppressing your thoughts?

_____

_____

_____

_____

_____

_____

_____

_____

_____

_____

_____

_____

_____

Competitive Anxiety

> *"YOU NEVER REACH YOUR FULL POTENTIAL BECAUSE YOU LET FEAR CONTROL YOUR THOUGHTS, AND THOSE FEARFUL THOUGHTS CREATE FEARFUL EMOTIONS, AND THOSE FEARFUL EMOTIONS LEAD TO FEARFUL ACTIONS."*

Mental Meltdown

Mental Meltdown

The moment you've been waiting for is just moments away. Everything you have worked for this entire season is on the line. All those countless hours of practice, all those early morning workouts and late night film sessions, the blood, the sweat, the tears, all the pain, agony, and defeat...all leading up to this moment. The division championship match.

How are you feeling? Sweaty palms? Butterflies or knots in your stomach? Are you finding it difficult to stretch and get loose? Looking up into the stands realizing how many people are there to watch you compete? Feeling the pressure of the moment?

Whether you're in a youth league or in the pros... young or old...a rookie or a veteran...competitive anxiety is experienced by every and all athletes at some point in their careers. And although experiencing some pre-competitive nerves is actually very normal, there are times where athletes become so overwhelmed that the anxiety cripples their thought process which in turn leads to a severe under performance.

But what exactly is this thought process? Well for starters, crippling anxiety is often a byproduct of an internal fear. This fear grabs control of the athlete's thoughts, and those fearful thoughts of course create fearful emotions, and those fearful emotions lead to fearful actions. It's a cycle that's very hard to break out of. But with the right training and mental approach you can limit the likelihood of experiencing high levels of competitive anxiety in the moments that mean the most to you and your team.

Definition and Examples

Competitive Anxiety- the nervous feeling you get before a big match, during a critical point in the match, and sometimes even after a match. Competitive anxiety is often something in your mind that you are "expecting" to happen, and that specific something causes you to be feel extremely nervous.

Along with Competitive Anxiety come two common outcomes, Fear of Failure and Choking Under Pressure.

1. *Fear of Failure-* an immense fear of taking chances, a fear of making mistakes, a fear of stepping outside of your comfort zone, a fear of losing, a fear of being unsuccessful, and a fear of the consequences that may follow.

   Example

   a. Sometimes at the end of practice coaches will select one runner to go around the track in a set amount of time. If the runner completes the lap in the allotted time, training for the day is over. But if the runner is unable to make the time, the entire team has to stay and do conditioning drills. Are you the one that steps up to take on the challenge, or do you fall back with no desire to take on the pressure? Are you afraid of the consequences that come along with you being unable to complete the lap in time?

2. *Choking (Choking Under Pressure)-* not performing as well as you normally do. In track and field, choking during crunch time is often associated with losing to a much slower

opponent, losing a competition after having a huge lead, giving up, and "shrinking" or shying away in the biggest moments of a competition.

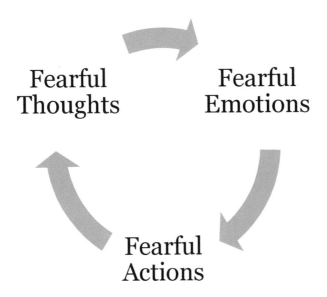

Fearful Thoughts

Fearful Emotions

Fearful Actions

The Game Plan

So what can you do to stop competitive anxiety from ruining your track and field career? What can you do to no longer experience that fear of failure that's stopping you from reaching your potential? And how do you avoid choking in the moments where it matters most for you and your team?

The first thing you must do is identify what it is that makes you nervous, what it is that makes you scared, and what it is that makes you underperform. Some of the most common influences that lead to increased levels of competitive anxiety might come as a surprise to you: friends, family, and even coaches and teammates. How so? Many young athletes become completely fixated on what the opinion of others would be if they were to have a bad performance. For example, what would your friends talk about at school the next day if you blew a huge lead in the final few yards of a race? How disappointed would your family be if you choked during the relay and missed the opportunity to put your team ahead? How nervous would you be to go to practice the next day knowing that your coach and teammates are furious that you didn't execute your long jump technique correctly and you didn't advance to the next round? If these things have ran through your mind in the past, not to worry, you're not alone! What's important for you to realize is that none of these outcomes are actually real! That's right I'll say it again, they're NOT REAL. They are all just thoughts that come across your mind all stemming from...yup you guessed it... FEAR. If you stopped thinking about the consequences and only focused on the task at hand the emotional response in your body would completely change. This outlook would in turn lower the amount of anxiety you experience.

Now, in some cases, some athletes experience anxiety, fear of failure, and choke under pressure because they've had an unsuccessful experience in the past. And this is a little bit different because when a similar experience arises, those thoughts resurface bringing along with them all the negative emotions and feelings that previously crippled the athlete into underperforming. However, there's also a distinction that must be made here which will undoubtedly change the outcome for these athletes. And here it is...Instead of thinking of past failures as obstacles, as insurmountable mountains, as impossible challenges...athletes should instead think of those failures as opportunities to learn, as chances to correct a mistake, as a second wind to blow past the competition. In doing so it would again change their entire thought process which makes all the difference. It's all a matter of perspective. You've only lost if you allow yourself to lose. Every failure you experience is a challenge that you can learn from, and the ability to apply that lesson to your immediate future is crucial to reach the level of success you so badly desire.

Mental Workouts

1. List your 3 favorite track & field athletes, go online and see what type of adversity and obstacles they have dealt with and overcame. How have they been criticized? What have they struggled with? How have they responded?

_____

_____

_____

_____

_____

_____

_____

_____

2. Now ask yourself the same questions above. How have you
    been criticized? What have you struggled with? How have
    you responded? And knowing what you know now, how
    would you respond differently?

_____

_____

_____

_____

_____

_____

_____

_____

_____

_____

Self- Talk

"SELF-TALK HAS BEEN SHOWN TO BE AN INCREDIBLY POWERFUL PSYCHOLOGICAL SKILL THAT IS USED BY SOME OF THE MOST SUCCESSFUL TRACK & FIELD ATHLETES."

Mental Meltdown

"How could I be so stupid? Why did I not make my move during the race when I had the chance? Why do I continue to practice even though it seems like I'm not getting any better? Maybe I should just quit?"

The comments/questions above represent a point in time where an athlete hits a brick wall and begins to negatively evaluate himself/herself in a way that is completely unproductive. Whether it's after not performing well during a competition, making a competitive mistake, or committing an error during practice...athletes across all sports experience these moments as they are nearly unavoidable, but nonetheless difficult to get through. And overall very little is done by coaches and trainers to correct these negative self-evaluations, which of course makes it extremely difficult for the athlete to ever realize it's a huge problem and a horrible habit that works against their favor. This unwanted problem and habit in turn has a direct negative impact on the athletes' performance.

This issue can be easily addressed by learning the mental skill (yes it is a skill), Self-Talk. And contrary to what you may believe...Self-Talk has been shown to be an incredibly powerful psychological skill that is used by some of the most successful athletes on the planet. There are some key distinctions however, so let's start by defining specifically what Self-Talk is and break it down into two different categories.

Definition & Examples

Self-Talk: speaking or talking to yourself out loud or in your thoughts.

Very straightforward. However, to ensure that athletes aren't negatively evaluating themselves and their performance, these two types of Self-Talk have become prominent.

Positive Self-Talk: telling yourself words, phrases, and affirmations to motivate you and keep you focused on your target.

Example

1. When I'm in the middle of a competitive matchup, I tell myself, "You can't beat me." "I'm too fast." "I can easily win."

2. "Hard Work Beats Talent When Talent Doesn't Work Hard"- commonly used quote.

Instructional Self-Talk: telling yourself instructions to make sure you're accomplishing your desired expectation.

Example

1. As you begin your triple jump approach you can recite to yourself "head down and push forward, drive with your knees up, and smoothly transition into the hop phase. Get as close to the pit as possible and launch." Exactly how your coach instructs you to do it during practice.

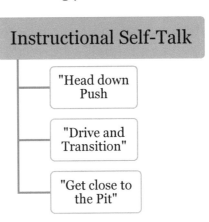

The Game Plan

It may seem strange to you that such a subtle change in the way you interpret and respond to your own behaviors and outcomes can make much of an impact on your athletic performance. But in reality, words are very powerful and really have a major influence in the way you view the world. Especially when we start considering how to deal with adversity, how to break through critical moments in your career, and how to continue to push when your gas tank is running on fumes...self-talk really becomes invaluable. A great example is non-other than David Payne, professional U.S. Olympic hurdler. If you're not familiar with his story, during a meet in Switzerland in 2013 he suffered a broken femur (the heaviest and strongest bone in the body). Many believed it was a career ending injury, including David himself...the injury was so severe that he pretty much had to learn how to walk again. It was devastating. As you can imagine, it was a very long road to recovery that really tested him both physically and psychologically.

And as you can guess...one of the key mental skills he relied on to help him in his rehab process was self-talk! If you get a chance to look up his story please do so it's truly very inspiring. He's documented saying that in certain moments he told himself "It's very depressing"... "You have to stop feeling sorry for yourself and go out there and so something about it"... "I'm not going to let this end my career." And slowly his thought process took a turn for the better... he went from believing he suffered a career ending injury to believing he had the ability to return to compete in the Olympics against the best in the world. Fortunately for David he was in fact able to re-learn how to walk, jog, and run again at an elite level. He fell just short of qualifying for the 2016 Olympics, but till this day he continues to be involved with the sport coaching other collegiate athletes and sharing his valuable experiences.

Lastly, whether you like the idea of using positive or instructional self-talk, my advice would be to use both, not one over the other. By using and developing both of these types of mental skills you certainly give yourself a huge edge over your opponents. It will allow you to prime your ability to stay focused which is really a lost art in todays' athletic world. In addition, it's highly recommended you start developing a "script." A script that you can use whenever you feel you need an extra boost in confidence or an extra push to get you over whatever hump you may be currently experiencing. Your script can come from anywhere, you can come up with it yourself or you can literally google "Motivational Quotes" and you'll find tons of short phrases that are designed to keep you focused and motivated. One thing is certain, you're going to be faced with great challenges throughout your career as a track and field athlete, no doubt about it. So it's best that when those challenges do arise and come your way you are ready to face them with the tools that'll give you the ability to overcome and conquer.

Mental Workout

1. Take some time and write down 10 words, phrases, and affirmations that get you focused. You can use anything that you've seen in a movie, read in a magazine, heard in a story, it can be something a friend has told you, advice from a teacher, whatever you'd like. Mix it up.

_____

_____

_____

_____

_____

_____

_____

_____

_____

_____

_____

_____

2. Put yourself in a competitive situation and think about where you can use self-instruction. Write down examples of what you would say to yourself. Write down as many examples as you can.

_____

_____

_____

_____

_____

_____

_____

_____

_____

_____

_____

Zones of Optimal Performance

> *"REACHING A MENTAL ZONE IS DIFFICULT, BUT WHEN ACCOMPLISHED MANY ATHLETES DESCRIBE THE EASE OF WINNING COMPETITIONS, DEFEATING OPPONENTS FEELS LIKE TAKING CANDY FROM A BABY, AND EVERY MOVE BECOMES BUTTERY*

Mental Meltdown

Take a moment and think back to a time where you witnessed your favorite athlete perform at an all-time high level. From Usain Bolt leaving other sprinters in the dust, to Carl Lewis winning Gold Medal after Gold Medal, to Michael Johnson winning Gold Medals for two different events in the same Olympic Games, (just to mention a few) there's been countless performances where athletes just leave fans in sheer awe and amazement. Seemingly every stride they take makes them stronger yet more relaxed, every move they make seems to create the necessary space and separation for them to build a huge lead, and everything just looks like they're light years ahead of the competition. And what do all these feats have in common regardless of the athlete who is performing them? At any of the post-race interviews you will undoubtedly hear them say…

"I was in a ZONE."

Reaching this "Zone" is one of the most prized objectives to all athletes regardless of the sport the athlete is participating in.

It's a state of mind where everything just starts to flow in their favor and things seem to come easy and natural. In track and field, many athletes describe the ease of winning competitions, defeating opponents feels like taking candy from a baby, and every move becomes buttery smooth. It's a beautiful thing to watch...and wouldn't it be more exciting if you as an athlete learned how you can reach this mental zone? Wouldn't it be great if you had the ability to replicate this phenomenon time and time again? Certainly your track and field performances would sky rocket! So our goal here is for you to take away some tips that'll help you understand where your personal zone of optimal performance lies in order for you to have the ability to implement the necessary skills required to reach this mental state.

Definition & Example

Zone of Optimal Performance- the level of anxiety that you perform best at, being able to reach a "mental zone", reaching a flow state, where everything just seems to come easy and you perform at your highest possible level athletically.

Example

1. During Usain Bolt's 2012 (2 gold medals) Olympic performance against some of the best athletes in the world it was evident from the start that he was in his own world. He set the entire sprinting world a blaze as he set new Olympic records seemingly with ease, and there was absolutely nothing anyone could do to stop him. During post-race interviews, Usain shed some light as to what he felt like during his legendary string of performances... making comments such as "I'm now a legend, I'm the greatest athlete to ever live"... "To all the people who doubted me, you can stop talking now. Bask in my glory." It's almost as if he had an out of body experience as he was so locked in to doing whatever it took to crush the competition and silence the doubters. Not even realizing that he was having one of the most remarkable performances in sports history.

The Game Plan

The possibilities of why Usain Bolt was able to record one of the greatest track and field performances of all time are really endless (since he's one of those athletes that are not from planet earth). However, from a sports psychology perspective there are a lot of factors we can break down that can tell us how and why some athletes can reach a mental zone and a flow state that allow them to perform at an abnormally high level. Some of these factors include being able to perform under pressure, being able to feel comfortable and relaxed, and getting over the fears of making mistakes during the course of a competition.

At the end of the day, many of the different factors all lead to one road...Learning to cope with Anxiety. Take a look at the Chart that follows.

The chart above shows a rough average of where athletes feel they perform best at in terms of level of anxiety (nerves). As you can see (the two highest points), most athletes perform at a high level when they are at an anxiety self-rating score of around 3 or a self-rating score of around 8. Scores near level 3 can best be described as moderately "low" anxiety while scores near level 8 can best be labeled as moderately "high" anxiety. And it all comes down to individual differences (personality, attitude, temperament, etc.). What does that mean? It means that some athletes simply prefer to perform under moderately low levels of anxiety because that's where they can perform best at. It's a level where they feel comfortable, it's a level where they feel dominant, and it's a level where they feel in control. And the same reasons go for the other athletes who prefer to compete under moderately high levels of anxiety. It's simply a matter of perspective and a matter of personal preference.

But let's consider the rest of the spectrum. Why don't athletes perform well at low anxiety self-ratings of 1 or high anxiety self-ratings of 10? Here's the answer…when athletes aren't nervous at all (anxiety self-rating of 1) they don't perform well because they're not excited, they're not motivated to perform, and they're not engaged in the activity they are doing. They simply start to go through the motions. Can you imagine competing in a division against 2-year old's? Sure you would be the best athlete in the competition, but it would be absolutely boring because it would be no contest! We all need to experience some level of nervousness to energize us and keep us focused. On the other hand, when athletes are really nervous (anxiety self-rating of 10) athletes panic, they psyche themselves out, and they start to freeze in the moment. Experiencing an enormous amount of anxiety all at once almost always leads to under-performing athletically. Not only that, but too much anxiety is also bad for your overall health, and can lead to a variety of different illnesses and mental health problems.

Now, after studying and learning the graph it's crucial for you to realize where you are along the spectrum. You have to know where you are in order to know how to progress and develop a "feel" for where your zone is. Are you a better performer under low levels of pressure and anxiety? Or do you prefer to feel higher levels of adrenaline when you compete? Only you can answer that. Once you figure that out, it's important for you to try and control (harness) this feeling so you can mimic (copy) the feeling every time you compete. For example, if you perform at your best when you have moderately low anxiety, then do everything you can mentally and physically to get into that same mental state. Establishing a routine works great for this! Eating your favorite comfort food before a competition…listening to your 10 favorite songs before practice…doing your favorite warm up drills before a tournament…there are many options. Finding what works for you will take some time and experimentation but will pay off greatly in the long run.

Mental Workout

1.   I want you to think back to a time when you performed at your absolute best. What did it feel like? Did you reach a mental "zone"? Was there a lot of pressure on you? How anxious or nervous were you before, during, and after the competition?

_____

_____

_____

_____

_____

_____

_____

_____

_____

_____

_____

2. Think back to a time when you performed at your absolute worst. What did you feel? Was there a lot of pressure on you? How anxious or nervous were you before, during, and after the competition?

_____

_____

_____

_____

_____

_____

_____

_____

_____

_____

3. Look back to your answers for questions 1 and 2. Do you
    notice any similarities between them? Do you notice any
    differences? What does this tell you about yourself?

_____

_____

_____

_____

_____

_____

_____

_____

_____

_____

_____

4. What are some things you can do before your next competition or before your next practice that will help put you in your zone of optimal performance? Also, go online and research the routines of your favorite track & field athletes. Are there some things that they do that you can use?

_____

_____

_____

_____

_____

_____

_____

_____

_____

_____

_____

_____

Attention

> *"WITH SO MANY FACTORS FIGHTING FOR YOUR ATTENTION YOU BECOME LIKE A SNIPER IN THE MIDDLE OF A WARZONE, YOU NEED TO BE ABLE TO FOCUS ALL OF YOUR ATTENTIVE ENERGY ON THE THINGS THAT MATTER MOST AT THAT VERY MOMENT."*

Mental Meltdown

It's finally race time! The gun goes off and all of your opponents get off to a really fast start in a sheer blink of an eye! Not to worry, there's still plenty of time left for you to make your move. Although you're in the middle of the pack right now you know you can make up for your slow start and catch up. As the next turn comes you make an attempt to cut into the lead but get a little too reckless and aggressive...bumping into one of the other competitors. You get the worst of it, lose your balance, and fall on the hard ground surface... and just like that you've lost all your momentum and have significantly decreased your chances to win the event.

During the course of a track and field competition there's an enormously large series of events going on all around you at the same time. You can practice as much as you possibly can, but there's simply nothing like competing in a real live event. You need to remember all the fundamentals your coach taught you during practice, you need to memorize all the bumps, twists, and turns in the particular course you're in, you need to react quickly if something un-anticipated happens during the competition, you need to know where your competitors are in relation to you, you need to be in perfect balance and keep a great pace throughout, and so on and so forth. It's very hard to keep up with it all. And not to mention that all this action is happening while your coach is yelling at you from the sidelines, your family and friends are screaming at you from the stands, and your teammates are all trying to get your attention whether they're on the course with you or on the bench. With so many factors fighting for your attention you become like a sniper in the middle of a warzone, you need to be able to focus all of your attentive energy on the things that matter most at that very moment.

D efinition and Examples

Divided Attention- trying to pay equal attention to many things at the same time (multitasking). Because your attention is divided, you don't perform as well as you would if you gave your full attention to one thing at a time.

Example

1. Steeplechase racing is one of the toughest and most challenging events for any athlete. It's difficult because decisions need to be made in a split second, communication with the training staff needs to be flawless, and the game plan needs to be very well understood as the way you run against one athlete may be different than the way you run against another (quick vs aggressive). Your attention must be laser like, as one small mistake can lead to a complete lapse which of course leads to a crushing loss.

a. *Inattentional Blindness-* this term explains the phenomenon of you not being able to see something that is very easily visible (obvious). You're unable to see it because of your lack of attention.

Example

1. When your coach instructs you to completely focus on exploding off the starting blocks during a hurdle relay, and you become fixated on doing exactly that. As you explode however, you don't time your steps properly to get over the first hurdle and end up having to come to a total stop. In plain view everyone could see that you wouldn't make it over the hurdle because of your stride,

but you became so fixated on exploding off the blocks that you didn't see it coming.

Selective Attention- being able to filter out information that isn't important, and focusing on the information that is important.

Example

1. While competing in a 100 meter sprint, being able to zone out all of the distractions and focusing on coming in first.

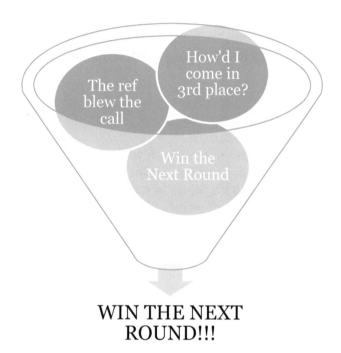

The ref blew the call

How'd I come in 3rd place?

Win the Next Round

WIN THE NEXT ROUND!!!

The Game Plan

The diagram above is a perfect depiction of how your mind can act like a filter or funnel during a race. Picture this: you hear the starter's gun and you're off to the races, one of the other competitors just slightly crosses over to your lane, you think he will be automatically be disqualified, but the judges failed to notice he obstructed your path and therefore no penalty is called. Worse, you come in third place and are now seeded lower in the rankings for the next round. In this situation it's easy to get distracted and divide your attention on how there should've been a disqualification or how you should've still placed higher. But what you should really be focusing your attention on is winning the next round of the event! It's just that simple. Yet so many times athletes get caught up into thinking how bad the referees are, or how much trash the other team is talking, or how the fans are being disrespectful. And when athletes get caught up with all the non-sense and different scenarios instead of being in the moment, that's when they end up under performing and getting benched. Don't let this be you.

Instead, utilize Selective Attention to zone in on the things that are most important in that moment, whether it's practice or a competition. Don't become a victim of divided attention and waste your attentive energy on multiple things that won't even help you perform at a higher level. And this doesn't only apply to track and field, think back to when you took your last algebra test, or your last biology exam... How many times did you catch yourself being distracted by something else that was completely unrelated to what you were doing.. like what you should eat for lunch, or what you're going to wear to the party, or how much clothes you should pack for your upcoming vacation? It happens to the best of us, and it's extremely unproductive. So understand that being able to focus on one thing at a time will enable you to give 100% effort on that one task, which will allow you to do it much more effectively and much more efficiently, leading to a much improved overall athletic performance.

 ental Workouts

1. Can you think of a competitive situation that you've encountered where you were asked to divide your attention on several different tasks? How did you feel? How did you perform?

_____

_____

_____

_____

_____

_____

_____

_____

_____

_____

_____

_____

2. Knowing what you know now, how can you use your attention more effectively?

_____

_____

_____

_____

_____

_____

_____

_____

_____

_____

_____

_____

Self-Confidence

> *"YOU ARE THE ARCHITECT, YOU CAN BUILD YOURSELF UP HIGH LIKE A SKYSCRAPER OR YOU CAN SET A FLIMSY FOUNDATION THAT CAN COLLAPSE AT ANY MOMENT."*

Mental Meltdown

It's the final stretch of the relay race, time slowly ticking away on the clock. Your team is in second place but just by a few meters...and guess who's up next to grab the baton??? That's right. YOU.

It's the most critical point in the race, a moment where you have the chance and power to dictate how it all ends. You can rise to the occasion and run your butt off to finish in first place, you can run hard and keep your position in second place, or you can completely blow it and allow the other sprinters to pass you up causing your team to lose a medaling position. What is the one thing every track and field athlete wished they had in this situation? SUPREME SELF-CONFIDENCE!

And yes...Confidence (or self-confidence) is one of the most important factors linked to the amount of success an athlete experiences throughout the course of their career. Why? The psychological and physical relationship is simple, the more confident you are mentally as a track and field athlete, the more likely you are to physically succeed and perform well. No matter how short you are, no matter how slow you are, no matter how untalented people say you are, if you're confident in your abilities you have a great chance of keeping up and competing with the best of them.

At the end of the day you are the architect, you can build your confidence up high like a skyscraper or you can set forth a flimsy foundation that can collapse at any moment. In other words, you are in charge of the level of self-confidence you hold within you...it really is all in your head! But if you lack the ability to build your confidence up, what happens is that as soon as you encounter a challenge or any type of adversity you will surely be unprepared and unequipped to deal with the added pressures that come along. So let's get a deeper understanding of what self-confidence really is and consider all the different factors that can influence the level of confidence you compete with.

Definition & Example

Confidence- having a strong belief in yourself and in your abilities.

Example

1. I'm confident that I'm the best athlete in the league this season.

A statement that is very easily said, but can be very difficult to prove. Especially as we consider the following confidence pitfalls:

If you are extremely quick but suffer a slightly sprained ankle, would you still have confidence in your speed? If you consistently knock down hurdles during warm ups, would you still have confidence in your hurdling ability during an actual competition? If your coach tells you you're not good enough to come in first place and not to get your hopes up, how confident would you be about your talents and abilities moving forward? There's too many confidence killing scenarios to name them all...what's important is to learn how to build and sustain high levels of confidence so that when your moment comes you are ready to perform at a high level.

The Game Plan

Here's lesson number one... there is a direct relationship between the amount of time you practice and the amount of confidence that you perform with. In other words, the more you practice the more confidence you will ultimately have. But pay close attention, when you're practicing and working on your skills you must ALWAYS start at the most BASIC LEVEL. Why? Because it's important to build a solid foundation before attempting to blossom to skill levels that you're unprepared for. For example, you might be guilty (as so many athletes are) of running onto the competitive field during warm ups and begin sprinting on the track or jumping on the high jump at full speed. Bad idea!

Instead what you should do is start by warming up at 50% effort, and then at 60% effort, and then 70% effort, and then 80% effort, followed by 90% effort, and then finally 100% full speed effort. It should be more of a steady progression warming your muscles up and getting a feel for your running or jumping technique. Going out and wildly performing at 100% and seeing yourself consistently miss your mark will only result in you feeling tentative and thinking "Damn I'm Off Today."

And it's not just for warm ups. Throwing, hurdling, long jumping, and any skill building activity for that matter should begin with the most simple and basic drills. A good example of this is Sydney McLaughlin's dynamic exercise routines prior to competing. As you've probably observed, even though she's one of the best collegiate hurdlers and sprinters in the country, she doesn't deviate away from doing her basic pre-event warm ups before each and every competition.

This leads us directly into lesson number two, Be a Student of the Sport. Study the skills and movements of collegiate, professional, and Olympic track and field athletes, or any athlete that is better than you for that matter. Watching someone who's better than you and being able to break down what they do in order to implement facets of their ability and technique into yours can be a huge confidence booster because you already know that what they're doing works. After all, they're better than you for a reason right? Mimicking these athletes is almost (and yes I said Almost) like having a short cut to success. They've put in years and years of hard work to develop and hone in on their skills and moves, and all you have to do is learn how to execute those moves yourself. Pro athletes do this all the time, just look at how Christian Taylor patterned his triple jump technique after Jonathan Edwards' technique as a young athlete. Great athletes constantly learn from other great athletes and simply follow the same path to success.

And finally lesson number three, and I can't stress it enough, is stay mentally resilient. As a track and field athlete, you are bound to be faced with adversity, you're bound to be faced with difficulties, and you are bound to make mistakes. That's just the nature of track and field. What makes the difference and what you need to concentrate on is how you react, how you bounce back, and how you are going to be better after the fact. As we've made this point before, no one has control over your thoughts and perception but YOURSELF. So keep grinding and don't let any outside noise interfere with your laser focus toward accomplishing your goals and aspirations.

 ## Mental Workouts

1. Think of a time when you competed with supreme confidence. Why did you perform with so much confidence? What were you thinking about? What was the outcome?

_____

_____

_____

_____

_____

_____

_____

_____

_____

_____

_____

_____

_____

2. Now do the opposite. Think of a time when you competed with absolutely no confidence. Why didn't you have confidence? What was going through your mind? What was the outcome?

_____

_____

_____

_____

_____

_____

_____

_____

_____

_____

_____

_____

_____

3. Analyze what you wrote for the two questions above. What can you do to perform with confidence all the time? On the other hand, what can you do to avoid losing your confidence during a competition?

_____

_____

_____

_____

_____

_____

_____

_____

_____

_____

_____

_____

Coming Back from Injury

> *"WHAT MOST ATHLETES FAIL TO REALIZE IS THAT THE PHYSICAL PAIN IS INTENSE, BUT TOLERABLE, IT'S THE PSYCHOLOGICAL PAIN THAT BECOMES ALMOST UNBEARABLE TO DEAL WITH."*

Mental Meltdown

It's Saturday morning and your coach sends a text to the entire track and field team...he's decided to have an early practice session in order to prepare for the tournament this upcoming weekend. Nothing intense, just an opportunity for everyone to work on the fundamentals and go over the game plan. A really light practice (and a dream come true)! Everything runs smoothly, and since there's nothing else to do once training is over, you and a couple of your teammates decide to stay late and have a little long jump competition amongst yourselves (despite your coach's advisement against it).

As the competition amongst your teammates begins everyone takes it very lightly and not serious at all. As natural competitors however, slowly but surely the competition begins to pick up building intensity with everyone competing harder and harder as your turns progress. Next thing you know during your turn as you plant your foot and prepare to spring off for your jump you feel as though someone kicked you on the back of your heel, causing you to collapse in intense pain. Just like that...you suffer a severe left Achilles injury and are out indefinitely for at least the next two weeks. No tournament for you!

Whether you like it or not, injury is a natural part of track and field. The sport itself is a wide series of events, taking place at very high intensities, with all athletes competing for the bragging rights of winning the first place medal or trophy. With intensity elevating at every level and with every athlete trying their hardest to win, someone is bound to get hurt or injured at some point even though it's unintentional. There's just too many things going on at the same time and risky situations all around. It's rare that any serious track and field athlete in the world escapes the injury bug entirely. And although we hope and pray for every athlete to have a good healthy career throughout, it's best that everyone is prepared and becomes equipped with the mental skills that are necessary to deal with and cope with the psychological and physical symptoms of an injury. From minor sprains to severely torn ligaments and broken bones, it's tough recovering and coming back at full strength. What most athletes fail to realize is that the physical pain is intense, but tolerable, it's the psychological pain that becomes almost unbearable to deal with.

"I'VE WORKED HARD OVER THE YEARS, I'VE BEEN INJURED AND I'VE WORKED HARD THROUGH IT, AND I'VE MADE IT."
-   USAIN BOLT

Definition & Example

Injury- being harmed physically, emotionally, and or psychologically.

Example

1. Injuries come in all shapes and sizes. In track and field, some of the most common injuries include sprained ankles, runner's knee, shin splits, pulled hamstrings and calf muscles, and lower back pain (just to name a few).

Now, when most athletes suffer from an injury they tend to focus on the physical injury itself. There may be a lot of swelling, significant muscle tightness, and overall the body needs time and rest in order to be able to fully recover. But the biggest downfall about this is that by not paying attention to the psychological aspects that an injury brings along with it...many athletes return from a serious injury when they truly aren't fully prepared or ready, and their performance on the competitive field suffers greatly. When an athlete isn't psychologically ready to return from an injury their thoughts are completely occupied on all the things that can possibly go wrong. They become afraid of re injury while attempting to get up and over that first hurdle, they become tentative in the movements they make as they gather to complete a high jump, they begin to second guess themselves and their ability while sprinting all out to finish a race, and they become scared to make that quick and explosive burst off the starting blocks while beginning an event.

Physical Recovery

Swelling
Muscle Tightness
Pain

Psychological Recovery

Frustration
Decrease in Confidence
Decrease in Motivation

The Game Plan

When it comes to injury, your primary concern should be of course PREVENTION. Wear protective gear like padding and braces, and make sure to warm-up and stretch properly before any physical activity. This way, the chances of you suffering a serious or severe injury will be significantly reduced. Which of course will save you a ton of pain and frustration in the future.

However in the event that you do suffer an injury, how can you recover in the fastest time possible both physically and psychologically? Well in terms of psychological recovery, in most instances the number one thing you will need to change in order to recover is your perception (the way you think about it). Many of today's young athletes make the unconscious decision to view their injury as an unfixable problem, as a mountain high obstacle, and as the end of their season or career. This in large part is due to many of the critics out there who make these insane claims that when certain injuries take place the athletes who have suffered them will never return to their old selves. That somehow, because of these injuries it becomes "impossible" to ever return to full strength... and athletes that choose to believe and perceive their personal situations this way actually recover the slowest and have the most difficult and painful recovery processes. How so? Well as we've mentioned before thoughts have an immense and direct impact on the body and how it responds. With that being said, as you've probably already guessed by now is that athletes who make the decision to view their injury as a challenge to get better, as a learning opportunity, as a chance to become smarter and stronger than before, and as a way to silence their doubters and critics once and for all are the ones who actually recover more quickly, efficiently, and effectively. So first you must re-frame your thoughts!

Secondly and importantly, it's necessary to have social support. For some of us I know it's extremely difficult to admit we need help let alone ask for help. But in terms of injury recovery it's crucial to have people around you that can support you when times get hard and when you start to get down on yourself, because at the end of the day the road will be tough! And in certain cases it may even be beneficial for you to seek help and support from those who are not associated in any way with your track and field career, like coaches, trainers, or teammates. Why? Sometimes, but not always, people who are tied to your track and field career may unintentionally put your athletic interest and ability first instead of your health and wellness. Meaning that they push and encourage you to return to competing regardless if you feel you're ready and recovered or not. Especially in youth sports, we often hear negative comments like "just suck it up, just walk it off, it's not that bad stop being a sissy..?" This is horrible advice. Not only do comments like these negatively impact an athletes psyche but they also leave athletes vulnerable to re-injury if they attempt to return to competing too soon.

Last but not least, a huge part of injury recovery must involve the mental skills you have learned in the previous exercises: mental imagery, positive/instructional self-talk, and goal setting. This is a perfect time for you to tie it all together. Visualizing yourself getting stronger every day, one step closer to full recovery, and setting short term goals to make sure you're reaching your target. You already know the science behind it, so I'll let you be creative and come up with your own mental skills plan.

 ## ental Workouts

1. Think about a time when you've been injured. What was your initial reaction? How did your reaction change over time? What was your recovery process like?

_____

_____

_____

_____

_____

_____

_____

_____

_____

_____

_____

_____

_____

2. Knowing what you know now, what would you do differently? How do you think your recovery process would have been different?

_____

_____

_____

_____

_____

_____

_____

_____

_____

_____

_____

_____

CPSIA information can be obtained
at www.ICGtesting.com
Printed in the USA
LVHW071516121221
705978LV00001B/9